CONDUCTING
EFFECTIVE
INTERVIEWS

Better Management Skills

This highly popular range of inexpensive paperbacks covers all areas of basic management. Practical, easy to read and instantly accessible, these guides will help managers to improve their business or communication skills. Those marked * are available on audio cassette.

The books in this series can be tailored to specific company requirements. For further details, please contact the publisher, Kogan Page, telephone 0171-278 0433, fax 0171-837 6348.

Be a Successful Supervisor
Business Etiquette
Coaching Your Employees
Consulting for Success
Counselling Your Staff
Creative Decision-making
Creative Thinking in Business
Delegating for Results
Effective Meeting Skills
Effective Performance Appraisals*
Effective Presentation Skills
Empowerment
First Time Supervisor
Get Organised!
Goals and Goal Setting
How to Communicate Effectively*
How to Develop a Positive Attitude*
How to Develop Assertiveness
How to Motivate People*
How to Understand Financial Statements
How to Write a Staff Manual
Improving Employee Performance
Improving Relations at Work
Keeping Customers for Life
Leadership Skills for Women

Learning to Lead
Make Every Minute Count*
Managing Disagreement Constructively
Managing Organisational Change
Managing Part-Time Employees
Managing Quality Customer Service
Managing Your Boss
Marketing for Success
Memory Skills in Business
Mentoring
Office Management
Productive Planning
Project Management
Quality Customer Service
Rate Your Skills as a Manager
Sales Training Basics
Self-Managing Teams
Selling Professionally
Speed Reading in Business
Successful Negotiation
Successful Telephone Techniques
Systematic Problem-solving and Decision-making
Team Building
Training Methods that Work

CONDUCTING EFFECTIVE INTERVIEWS

John Fletcher

KOGAN
PAGE

Thanks to Francis Burley who gave invaluable help.

First published in 1995

Kogan Page Limited
120 Pentonville Road
London N1 9JN

© John Fletcher 1995

British Library Cataloguing in Publication Data

A CIP record for this book is available from the British Library.

ISBN 0 7494 1438 3

Typeset by BookEns Ltd, Royston, Herts.
Printed and bound in Great Britain by Clays Ltd, St Ives plc

278443

Contents

CHAPTER 1
Principles of Interviewing

What is an interview?

An interview is a discussion between two people to achieve a purpose. This is the definition of an interview used in this book. Although interviews usually take place between a boss and a subordinate at work, the principles of effective interviewing apply to most meetings where two people are trying to achieve something by discussions. Panel interviews are a special case that will be looked at later (page 38).

If the interview does not have a well-defined purpose it simply becomes a conversation. In the same way, a purposeful conversation is in effect an interview. Interviews can easily slip into mere conversations if they stray from their purpose. Much of the anxiety that is felt about an interview would disappear if it was thought of as just a purposeful discussion. By the time they start working people have had years of experience of conversations. They discover what is effective in getting their point over and what amuses people. They learn about the subtle nonverbal signals that people give out if they are interested or bored, and some people become quite good at handling difficult people or subjects.

All this experience is invaluable preparation for interviewing at work. It is true that not everyone finds conversation easy, and this is often because they cannot think of what to say. That is not a problem for you as an interviewer; the purpose dictates what needs to be covered. If the purpose has been achieved, or if it is agreed that it cannot be achieved, then the interview should end.

If you are faced with planning and preparing for an interview, start by thinking about the purpose. This will help you to abandon some of your assumptions or anxieties about the interview, and help you to be more creative in planning your interview and more effective at carrying it out.

Interviews are often thought of as 'formal' occasions. What exactly does this mean? Take a moment to write down what you think of as defining a 'formal' interview.

You may have written something like:

- Official occasion
- In an office
- Taking notes
- Applying for a job.

A formal interview may be all these things, but more important, it does not have to be any of them. You might plan a very useful interview at work in the canteen, during a break, or even after work in the pub. 'Formal' does not have to mean 'official'; for example, you may be more effective in your interview by not taking notes.

Just to confuse matters, bear in mind that some organisations use the phrase 'formal interview' in a different way. For example, an initial disciplinary interview might be called 'informal' but a written record is nonetheless kept of the fact that it took place. A second interview might be called a 'formal disciplinary' interview. If you are not sure about the rules for disciplinary interviews check with your personnel department. The rules can vary from one company or organisation to the next.

Planning and preparation

Managers rarely achieve their goals without planning. If you are to achieve your purpose in an interview, you need to plan it too. Start by deciding the purpose, aim or outcome that you want. All other practical preparation flows from that decision. Typical aims for an interview are:

- To improve someone's performance
- To gauge or improve morale, motivation or attitudes
- To give or receive information
- To allow the subordinate or the boss to air their views or 'let off steam'
- To improve systems, procedures or implement a new policy
- To clear up misunderstandings
- To find out how successful the last interview was.

If you are planning an interview in the near future, write down the purpose or aim in one short, clear sentence.

Practical preparation for your interview

This section gives you some basic guidelines for planning your interview. Use the space after each subsection to make notes for your particular interview.

1. Clarify in your mind the exact purpose of the interview.
   - Don't try to achieve something that would be better done by a larger meeting, memo or a circular.
   - Avoid setting a purpose that is unrealistic in the time available.
   - Make sure that your purpose is something that you personally have the authority to carry through (particularly in disciplinary or grievance interviews).

2. Do your homework.
   - Get the necessary background information and facts.
   - Give advance notice to your interviewee.
   - Book a suitable place, if possible where you will not be interrupted.
   - Make a list of the main points you need to cover.
   - Anticipate any problems, conflicts of interest or motive that you might come up against.

3. Plan the timing.
   - Allocate enough time in your day planner or diary.
   - Make sure that you will not be interrupted, and let others know when you expect to be available.
   - Make sure you can see a clock or watch easily during the interview.

4. Outline your plan for the discussion.
   - Think through your opening statement or question.
   - Try to predict the other person's initial reaction.
   - Plan the main stages of the interview, and how long each should take.
   - Determine what you would like to be the final stage or summary of the interview.
   - Identify stages in the interview where you might have to modify your outcome depending on what you are told.

5. Problem-solving interviews.
   - Review the cause of the problem, not just its symptoms.
   - Identify all possible solutions.
   - Consider the implications of each possible solution.
   - Pick the best one.
   - Keep an open mind – listen to the ideas of others.

6. Have everything ready.
   - Choose a suitable place for the interview.
   - Ensure privacy.
   - Prepare any supporting documents, stationery, pens, access to equipment, etc.
   - Give notice to your boss, staff or assistant that you will not be available until after the interview.

The structure of the interview

The next 30 points or so are not all equally important, nor do they all apply to all interviews. Failure to recognise the importance of some of them will mean the interview is not fully professional. Neglect of others could mean disaster.

Think which will apply to your interviews.

Introduce the main topic
- State the main topic you want to discuss and the outcome you want to achieve.
- State the time available.
- Explain how much response you expect from the other person.
- Provide any background information you have.
- Ask for background information from the other person.
- Check the facts and the main points.
- Clarify the scope of the interview: what you can discuss and any topics you cannot discuss.
- Set the tone for the interview.
- Make clear that you want to listen as much as talk.
- State if the conversation will be confidential, or recorded, or if you want to take notes.
- Outline what you see as the logical path or sequence for the interview.

Guide the discussion
- Agree the nature and style of the discussion, and adjust this if required as the conversation develops.
- Draw out as much information as you can from the other person.
- Distinguish subjective opinion from hard facts, and clarify the facts as you go.
- Restate any contentious views in your own words.
- Repeat and adjust this if necessary until the other person agrees.
- Clear up any misunderstandings as you go.
- Stay on target: avoid being side-tracked.
- Discourage (or simply ignore) personal remarks about you or third parties. Stick to facts.
- Separate reason from emotion.
- Encourage the other person to talk and explain their view (you don't have to agree with it, but you need to know what it is).

- Keep an eye on the time and your time plan.

Clarify and crystallise the process
- Summarise each stage of the interview.
- State any intermediate conclusions that are reached.
- Clarify any points of disagreement.
- Check that summaries are understood and agreed at each stage.

Establish and check the results of the interview
- Give a final summary from your point of view.
- State what you feel has been agreed and what (if anything) still needs to be resolved.
- State if you feel a further interview is needed.
- Check that your summary has been understood.

Status and rights

Everyone has rights at work irrespective of their position or status. Respect other people's rights and dignity during any interview. This includes the rights of any third parties as well as the rights of the person you are talking to.

Your interviewee has a right:
    to courtesy
    to be heard
    to be taken seriously

(and so do you).

Third parties have a right:
    not to be misquoted
    not to be 'run down'

(and so do you).

The manager who opens an interview with a statement such as 'Well, I know that senior management are all keen on this, but it will probably blow over soon, flavour of the month it seems to me', cannot expect much respect from their staff, nor from senior management when they find out (as they inevitably will). Any boss who is not loyal to their management cannot expect much loyalty from their staff.

Clarify responsibilities

In any organisation everyone needs to know who is responsible for what if you are going to make much progress. Beware of undermining the allocation of responsibility — you risk defeating the purpose of your interview. Ensure that you clarify the limits of everyone's responsibilities. When delegating, bosses retain the responsibility for what is done, even if they delegate the authority for getting it done to a subordinate. This can seem to some bosses like taking an enormous risk. This sense of risk can be transformed into good management if both parties know what they should be doing, and when and how they should meet again to check on progress.

Truth and sincerity

In Roman times if the mould for a bronze statue was accurately cast it was a true reflection of the original and it did not need any touching up with wax before the final casting. It was described as *sine-cere* (without wax). Make sure that your approach to interviewing is the same, that it is a true reflection of the matters in hand. Few will listen seriously to a source of information they think is untrustworthy.

For example, if someone asks why they were not promoted, you might find it easier at the time to prevaricate a little, or give a plausible reason that is not the whole truth: 'Ah well, you are not really qualified for that job, you see.' You will have a real credibility problem when they reappear in six months' time with the relevant qualification and repeating their request for promotion.

The best argument against short-term deceptions (even

those made with the best of intentions) is the prospect of the mopping-up interview afterwards. The aim of an interview must be legitimate. Managers who try to justify deceptions or half-truths on the grounds that the end justifies the means will find that in the long run they will not have done themselves any favours. Beware of the wax in insincere motives for any interview at work.

Communication without words

Three-quarters of the information we get from another person comes through our eyes rather than our ears. Sincerity in an interview means that the non-verbal messages should match the verbal ones. If you doubt the power of non-verbal messages, try watching a TV soap opera and see if you can follow the story with the sound turned down. You will be surprised how much information is still accessible. The power of non-verbal communication in an interview lies with whoever realises its value and uses it carefully.

Non-verbal messages
To reinforce your words consider some of the non-verbal messages you can send:

- silences
- grunts, 'ers' and 'ums' of agreement (or disagreement)
- facial expressions
- head nodding (to encourage the other person to continue)
- appearance (smart, casual, informal, official, etc)
- posture (eg leaning forward to show interest)
- holding eye contact (not for too long, to show you are listening)
- variations of voice
  - lowering the volume for emphasis (often more effective than raising your voice)
  - using pauses and deliberate hesitations (to allow the other person time to respond)
- humour (cheerfulness or to release tension).

Cues for friendliness and encouragement

In any meeting non-verbal cues can be used to encourage or discourage the other party. Frequently you will want to make the atmosphere more relaxed and friendly, build up the other party's confidence and improve relations between you. Try these:

- leaning forward or sitting forward in your chair
- removing physical barriers such as desks
- coming round to sit side by side (to look at documents, etc)
- setting chairs at right angles (informal but not casual)
- offering refreshments, such as coffee or soft drinks (it is hard for the other party to maintain a strong negative posture while holding a cup).

Cues for discouragement or control

On some occasions you may want to discourage the other person; you may want to control them or limit the time they take up. All these make it harder for the other party to communicate with you:

- frowning, disagreeing and interrupting
- talking too fast
- ignoring feedback or questions
- changing the subject abruptly
- giving orders rather than listening
- avoiding eye contact.

These two ways of behaving, positively encouraging and negatively controlling, provide a framework for control: appeal and hidden threat, reward and social punishment. Friendliness and sympathy are rewards; people like to feel welcome. Withholding friendliness can be used to maintain distance and make the other person work harder to get their message across (useful for dissuading unwelcome sales representatives!). They should be used with care, particularly the negative cues, as anyone who feels they are being manipulated will tend to resent it. In some interviews you can afford to ignore the feelings you create in the other person, but in interviews at work with colleagues or subordinates bear in mind that you need their cooperation, and you could endanger that by being distant or manipulative.

Keeping control of the interview

You should practice ways of controlling the discussion without seeming to dominate it. You need control of the direction and timing of the conversation without creating resentment. The five main factors in the control of an interview are:

1. the relative amount of talking by each party
2. the tempo or pace of the interview
3. the degree of freedom allowed
4. the digression or side-tracking that is tolerated
5. the level of emotional expression or relaxation.

For instance, in an investigative or factual interview you might aim to:

- stay strictly on track
- only accept hard facts or information
- minimise the degree of emotion expressed.

Whereas in an appraisal interview you would want to:

- listen more than you contribute
- encourage feelings to be aired
- accept that subjective views are as valid as historical facts.

In a grievance or disciplinary interview you could gain a lot from:

- asking your interviewee to explain their side first
- letting them elaborate in their own words
- allowing them to overstate their case and thus perhaps see the weakness of their own argument for themselves.

It is often more effective to maintain an impartial attitude than to use your authority to ram home your own view.

Using questions

The interviewer's main instrument of investigation and control is the carefully phrased question. The person asking the most questions not only controls the exchange but learns the most from it. Use questions:

- to encourage people to explain themselves ('I'd like to hear how you saw it')
- to draw out detail or admissions ('Can you tell me more about ...?')
- to amplify facts and opinions ('So what happened next?')
- to keep the discussion on track ('Hmm, I see, but how does that relate to ...?')
- to reintroduce a point that was overlooked or skirted ('Going back to the cost of it, what effect would this have on the budget?')
- to check emotional expression ('I understand you were very upset, but what exactly did he say?').

Take care not to phrase your questions in a way that implies criticism or gives away your personal judgement. Judgement can be given later if it is relevant. First you need to get the facts. For example, 'Well, that wasn't wise was it?' is hardly going to encourage further explanation, whereas the neutral 'What was the effect of what you did?' is likely to get to more relevant detail.

Opening up and closing down questions
Questions that start with Who, Where or When tend to get you facts or short replies, although they will close down the exchange. Questions that start with Why, How or What open up the conversation. Such 'open' questions can be very useful if they are also limited by constraints. These are sometimes called 'funnelling' questions. Use them to guide your

interviewee without controlling them: 'So, in terms of the staffing, what would the implications be?' This question sets the subject (staffing) but leaves the other person free to express themselves.

Difficult people and topics

If you have an interview to prepare that covers a difficult subject, or means you will have to interview a touchy person, make a list of the difficulties that your interviewee may give you.

You may have listed:

● being over-talkative
● bringing in irrelevances or straying from the main topic
● being impatient or too emotional to be rational
● having a closed mind
● being dogmatic or making wild accusations or statements
● being more concerned with scoring points than making progress
● not listening or being preoccupied.

The temptation is to take such problems personally and imagine that the interviewee simply does not want to talk to you. The chances are that if they are really angry or upset they would not talk rationally to anybody.

1. Do your best to de-personalise the discussion, by aiming to correct the problem rather than the interviewee's personality or character.
2. Stick to the facts not the emotions; constantly bring them back to the agenda you have set for the interview.
3. In extreme cases adjourn the interview, giving your reason in impersonal terms. That is, it is not that you don't want to talk to them but you want to restart the interview when you have both had time to reflect.

Traps for the unwary

In highly charged emotional interviews (the type of interview often thrust upon you at short notice) beware of:

- taking things personally
- siding against a third party to express sympathy with the interviewee
- accepting statements without access to the facts or the other side of the story
- criticising the company, other departments, the opposition, or anyone else
- expressing your own values or judgements (other than company policy if it is relevant).

If you remain impartial, objective and sincere you will avoid the traps that would leave you with a second interview that may well be more difficult to handle than the first!

Controlling anxiety

People who feel defensive, anxious or under threat rarely express themselves clearly. Conversely, those who are over-confident or too relaxed might belittle the serious concerns and overlook questions that need to be answered. If the anxiety level is too high you need to reduce it to a level that enables a reasonable exchange of views. If the anxiety level is too low, you need to introduce some concern to ensure that questions get the airing they deserve.

To reduce the anxiety level you must convey trust and control any tendency to prejudge. Allow adequate time so that the interview is not rushed, and above all be seen to listen with care. Do this by:

- showing signs of concern or even affection
- giving reassurances (but only those you know you can commit yourself to)
- allowing the other person time to talk

- focusing on them and minimising distractions
- restating what has been said to clarify understanding
- giving non-verbal cues of listening (eye contact, nods, etc).

To increase the level of concern or anxiety, try to convey both the seriousness of the topic and the importance or formality of the interview. Make them aware of your authority as the boss, and even the implications if the interview fails in its purpose. Do this by:

- sticking to the facts
- being unemotional
- increasing your distance (mentally and physically)
- being precise and accurate in your phrases
- being sharp and to the point if necessary
- clarifying any options or conflicts for the interviewee.

Reflective summarising

Reflective summarising is so effective as an interview technique it almost feels like cheating. This is simply stating back to the other person a summary of what they have just said. In this way you encourage them to continue, prove that you are listening and can check that you have understood, all at the same time. The technique is much used in counselling but beware of overusing it or your subordinate will think that the interview is taking place in an echo chamber.

Statement: He's just not interested in being helpful, I think he's got something against me.
Restatement: You feel he has got a grudge?
Statement: Not exactly a grudge, but ever since I got the new job he has had a bad attitude.
Restatement: A bad attitude?
Statement: Yes, always the last to help out, and often moaning about the work share.

Reflective summarising, or restating, can be a very powerful tool in interviewing, if it is used correctly. Bear in mind these rules:

- Don't echo the interviewee – use your own words or tone of voice.
- Don't 'read between the lines' or guess at what has been unsaid.
- Allow time for a reply – your interviewee may be groping for words.
- If you are restating facts, sum up the main points rather than repeat every detail.
- If you are restating feelings or beliefs, simply restate them without adding any judgement of your own.

Allow for the possibility that you have misunderstood by indicating that you are not certain in your views. A typical summary might be: 'So by then you were feeling pretty angry, is that right?', 'It seems to me that you felt ....

Redefining

At the start of any interview you should make sure that your interviewee understands the purpose or aim of the interview. Sometimes it turns out that the aim changes during the course of the interview due to new information or a clarification of the facts. One problem may turn out to have several facets, or prove to be insoluble in the time available. If that happens you should redefine the purpose, reset the agenda for the interview, and make sure that your interviewee accepts the new aim. For example, an interview about stock losses might take an unexpected turn and you may have to redefine the aim: 'When we started I thought we were looking at poor stock-control procedures, but from what you have said, it seems this is simply theft. Now if that is the case, we need to stop and rethink ...'

In emotionally charged interviews, redefining can help to focus on the problem and reduce the emotional or irrational content. The words state the facts; the tone will set the emotional level. If a subordinate has requested a grievance interview, redefining the purpose means you can remove any personal hostility from the exchange and focus on the problem rather than the personal aspects. You will need to get this definition accepted with a question such as, 'So have I covered all the main points you want taken into account?'. Your subordinate is unlikely to add, 'No, there is also the fact that I simply hate that person!'.

Redefining is a special case of restating. It can serve you as an intermediate summary and act as a starting-point for the problem-solving stage of the interview.

CHAPTER 2
The Selection Interview

What should selection interviews achieve?

The purpose of the selection interview is to help to choose the right people for jobs by:

- informing applicants about the job
- predicting which applicants will be willing and able to do the job
- influencing suitable applicants to accept the post
- creating a good impression of the organisation to all the applicants.

Remember that the selection interview is poorly named in that it is really an information exchange interview. The selection decision itself will come after all the candidates have been interviewed, and when the information gained about them has been evaluated according to the job description and personal profile.

Difficulties you may face

There are particular difficulties in conducting a selection interview.

1. It can be a a tense time for both parties, who each have a

lot at stake. The applicant wants the job, and the employer wants the right person. There will be more applicants than jobs, and this just adds to the tension.

2. Both parties are on their best behaviour. Each side will want to emphasise their good points and draw a veil over their weaknesses. The 'best' applicant may just be good at being interviewed rather than the best person for the job.

3. Even a long interview is a short time for an interviewer in which to predict how the applicant will perform over the coming years.

4. An interview is a subjective process, and is unreliable. It is hard to be totally objective about people when we first meet them and the selection interview is no exception. We are all biased or prejudiced to some degree, and it seems impossible to overcome our 'gut feelings' of people, even though experience tells us that first impressions can mislead.

5. It is easy to be faced with a pleasantly outgoing candidate and conclude that they are honest, trustworthy and generally respectable. This is the so-called 'halo effect'; confidence tricksters rely on the human failing that many people will draw conclusions about the whole from an unrepresentative sample. The 'cloven-hoof effect' is the same thing in reverse. For example, you may infer that a candidate with scruffy shoes is likely to have poor standards in other ways too. If the post calls for someone who makes a good first impression, information about their initial appearance may be of value, but on the whole these judgements are best kept until later.

Preparing for the interview

The aim of a selection interview is to gain information to help to choose the right candidate. The whole selection process should start long before the interview and include these steps:

1. Long-term organisation planning. Every manager should have a projected organisation chart for the next five years,

showing what kind of organisation they are aiming to be, and what kind of people they will need. Like most organisation charts, it will need continuous amendment and will always be slightly out of date. However, every selection should be made with an eye to compatibility with this long-term plan. If you have not got a long-term plan, make a note to ask your manager about one.

2. A list of the factors of your long-term plan that you should be considering in particular.

3. Advertising. This is the first filter in your selection process. Draft and present your job announcements in a way that appeals most to the type of person you are looking for. List the factors you would want to project in your advertisements. Bear in mind that an advertisement that produces hundred of replies may not have described the job or your requirements accurately. The ideal advertisement attracts a few dozen suitable applicants.

Job description

The main purpose of the job description in selection interviewing is as a checklist to help you to prepare. It makes sense to have a clear definition of the job before advertising for, and selecting, the applicants to match it. In reality the process does become two-way, and sections of the job description may later become subject to negotiation. Recent practice is to try to make the job fit the person as much as finding an ideal person to fit the job. Many companies hire graduate trainees for example, and only later determine which department or speciality they might work in.

Job descriptions evolve as well as people. Technical innovation alone means that most managers should revise their staff's job descriptions regularly. Due to the pace of change at work the relative importance of the items in the job description can change too. An attribute that was previously merely desirable (such as a foreign language or keyboard skills) might become necessary for the position.

Some posts are advertised by 'achievement areas', or 'key

results areas'. These are essentially the main duties of the post written as outcomes rather than tasks. This takes a more positive approach to selection, and is a good way of styling advertising to attract someone with a positive, achieving outlook. Achievement areas should not be prioritised: satisfactory job performance means that all the areas need to be achieved. This is similar to the concept of the National Vocational Qualifications (NVQ) competence performance criteria, where all the criteria are considered equal for the competent performance of the job.

Personal profile

There are a number of approaches to writing a personal profile. These are usually based on the five-, seven- or even nine-point plans and usually result in the clumsily named 'person specification'.

There is a simple, easy-to-remember system that just asks a two-part question: 'Are they *able and willing* to do the job?'. Abilities can be measured outside the interview, whereas willingness, enthusiasm or interest is usually assessed during the interview. The answer to this two-part question gives you a personal profile of the ideal candidate that will allow you a careful and focused preparation for the interview itself.

It would hardly be possible to construct a useful profile from a job description alone: you need to consider the abilities and attitudes that the ideal job-holder would need. The personal profile forms the basis of the questions for your interview, ability tests, reference follow-ups and any other checks you will need to make on the applicant's experience and qualifications.

There are several ways to assess ability, but hardly any alternatives to the interview for assessing willingness. In theory there are references, but their value is variable. We will look first at non-interview testing, and then at references, before examining ways of selecting able and willing recruits.

Assessing ability outside the interview

If the job calls for specific abilities that you are unlikely to assess in an interview, you may want to consider specialist ability tests. Film actors submit to screen tests and bricklayers build 'test walls'. Ability tests exist for just about every mental ability or disposition you could wish to name. Many of these tests can only be applied, and the results interpreted by trained specialists.

Start by listing the abilities you might want to measure in your ideal candidate. If any of the items on your list are essential for the job, and are difficult to assess in an interview, ask yourself how you are going to measure these abilities.

Problems with references

- They depend a lot on the referee. Some take the task seriously but a few do not.
- Most referees are well known to the applicant and hesitate to say anything critical.
- The skilful reference reader learns to look for what is conspicuous by omission, although there is the risk that the writer merely forgot.
- Occasionally references are worthless, as glowing tributes simply designed to help candidates on their way.
- Some are simply too ambiguous to be useful, for example, 'Any manager would be lucky to get Mr Smith to do the accounts.'

Are the candidates able?

Are they physically able?

Make a list of the physical abilities and attributes that your job holder will need to be competent in the job. The points to consider are:

- Have they got the strength, stamina and relevant physical capabilities?
- Is a favourable first impression an essential requirement, such as physical coordination or good posture? (Could you

really justify any selection decisions based on this?)
- Is any skill so important that you should consider a separate ability test outside the interview?
- The ability to attend work at short notice, or unsociable hours, may be important. Bear in mind for your interview planning that any questions should focus on the ability, never on assumptions based on the personal circumstances of the candidate.
- List the activities you might reasonably expect someone to be good at if they met all your physical requirements. Include any physical aspects of previous employment that you believe to be relevant.

Are they mentally able?
Does your candidate have intelligence, knowledge, experience, skills and judgement to do the job? Do they need to be able to make fine judgements or to be original and creative? Make a list of the mental abilities and attributes that your job holder will need to be competent in the job. The points to consider are:

- What academic qualifications would they probably have? Would qualifications alone give a reliable indication of real ability?
- Are there any abilities or specialist mental skills so important that you should test for them separately?
- What professional training should they have had, or be willing to take?

List the subjects, topics or interests that your candidate might have experience in if they are likely to have the mental skills for which you are looking. Beware of assuming that this list is exclusive, and plan to ask the candidate if they have similar interests.

Are the candidates willing?
In most interviews you can safely assume that candidates want the job; what you need to find out for selection purposes is

why they want it. What is their motive or ambition? At the end of your selection process, willingness or motivation might be the 'tie breaker' between two otherwise equally well-qualified applicants. Consider the following:

- Do you want someone to be satisfied with the present job, or someone with career ambitions?
- Do you need someone who is people-oriented or task-driven?
- Does your organisation offer tangible or social rewards, and what kind of person will be motivated by those rewards?
- Are money and financial status important to the applicant? Will they be disappointed?
- Does your organisation have a strong philosophy about its work and purpose? Is the applicant likely to share that philosophy?
- Will your applicant have to push and try hard in the job? Could someone with too much energy do the job well?
- Do you need someone who is cautious or courageous, rigid or flexible, a rebel or a conformist?
- How much effort should they have put into previous jobs (or at school) to be the type of person you are looking for?

Again, make a list of relevant previous activities and results that you might expect your ideal applicant to have achieved. As before, bear in mind that your best candidate may not have done any of the things you have listed, so plan to ask them about similar activities or results.

Fairness and equality

You need to review your profile to ensure that there has been no trace of unintended discrimination. There are two good reasons for this. First, you could miss out on the best applicant for your job; and secondly, selection on grounds that cannot be justified is illegal. Discrimination is also bad for your organisation's reputation. If your employment criteria fall in a sensitive area then take professional advice, but common sense and simple fairness are usually reliable guides.

The main rule of thumb is to make sure you are planning to obtain information in your interview on the skills or attributes that the candidate will need to do the actual job. The emphasis here must be on the relevance to the job.

It is reasonable to:
ask all your candidates if they can attend work at certain times.

It is not reasonable to:
ask only some of them if they have children to look after.

It is reasonable to:
select on ability in a relevant language.

It is not reasonable to:
suppose that only certain nationals or groups speak that language.

It is reasonable to:
assess someone's attitudes and cultural awareness if a certain outlook is a pre-requisite of the job.

It is not reasonable to:
avoid certain applicants because you feel they may not be acceptable to other employees or customers.

It is reasonable to:
enquire if candidates are physically able to do the task.

It is not reasonable to:
reject certain candidates because they require reason-able adaptations to allow them to work.

Finally, remember that there is a temptation, in looking for the best candidate, to over-specify the person you need. Such a candidate might walk into the job, walk all over it and walk out when there is no further challenge to them, leaving you looking for someone else, often at short notice.

Review your interview planning, and make a final note of any selection criteria that you cannot justify. This is the time to challenge any unconscious assumptions you may have made about your potential recruit's profile.

Final preparations

Most interviews are about half an hour to an hour. This is not a long time to make an assessment about someone who may be working for you for years to come. You should review your planning to make the best use of the interview time.

Review the profile
A useful method is to list the factors on your personal profile, marking the importance of each factor, and then make a copy for every applicant. You can use these to review what you know of the applicant so far, and add to it during the interview. The more consistent you are in this the easier it will be to make comparisons later.

Review the papers at hand, such as application form, references, accompanying letters and CV:

- What evidence is there for matches to your selection factors?
- Are there any serious omissions?
- Is there anything that you do not understand (an obscure job title for example)?
- Is there anything you want confirmed, or that you want more details about?
- Are there any discrepancies you want to explore, or information that points to the applicant being unsuitable?

Finally, make a note of any interesting points that would make for a comfortable or easy opening to the interview.

Interview structure

Beginning
Job applicants are often nervous; they may feel that the encounter is rather artificial or that they are undergoing some kind of test. None of this is of much benefit to you as the interviewer, as you are not seeing the sort of behaviour that they would probably show in the job. Your first task,

therefore, is to enable them to provide what you need — impartial information.

After welcoming the candidate and thanking them for coming to see you, a useful ploy is to offer some form of refreshment, typically a cup of coffee. Many people unwind with a coffee break, and this association can help them to feel relaxed. The simple ceremony of the cup and spoon is familiar socially, and offers you the chance to comment on a neutral topic, such as the quality of the coffee, the distance they had to travel, or whatever. Bear in mind that some candidates may not know whether they should drink or not during the interview. Offer then an unspoken guide by either sipping your own cup, or firmly putting it aside with a 'Right then, to move to ...'.

Probes

Your main purpose is to gain information to enable you to take a later decision. This is where you need to ask questions, and probe if necessary to get the information you need. Bear in mind that care may be needed as candidates will hesitate to reveal some facts, and all will be trying to portray themselves in what they see as their best light.

A successful way of gaining information is to use the 'sheepdog' questioning technique. Start with a statement, or a detail taken from the application form, and phrase your questions to guide the conversation to the facts or outcome that you are interested in. (See page 19.) For example, your candidate has stated that they took part in contractual negotiations, and you want to know exactly what their role was. The exchange might go like this:

You: I see you were in the team involved in the Conglomerated Widgets take-over negotiations.

Candidate: Yes it was most interesting, a very valuable experience.

You: What part did you play?

Candidate: I was involved all the way through. It took weeks of work.

You: So it was a long job. Were you actually heading the team taking the decisions?

Candidate: Well no, my boss headed the team; I took all the notes for her.

You: So although you saw all the action, you were not personally responsible for the final outcome?

Candidate: No, my role was administrative really.

Notice that in using the sheepdog technique it is useful to:

- start by checking your basic facts or topic area
- not be too easily satisfied if your probing questions are not clearly answered
- reflect back what the candidate says (this shows you are interested, and confirms progress as you go along)
- finish with a closed question (inviting a yes or no reply) to confirm the essential fact you are after
- avoid making the conversation sound like an interrogation
- make sure that your checking questions are at least softened by a courtesy or an explanation.

In this example the candidate was possibly hoping to give the impression that they had a more important role than they really did, but it can work the other way too. Some people are naturally modest and by probing you may find they are hiding their light under a bushel.

You: So it was a long job. Were you heading the team taking the decisions?

Candidate: Well yes, the take-over was my idea in the first place really, so the Director handed over the whole job to me. I had about 15 accountants on my team in the end.

The job
The applicants will want to find out about the job when they visit you, and the next stage of the interview should be a review of the job to encourage any questions they have. Much

of the job information can be given out before the interview in the job description or by letting the candidates meet existing employees.

Take care not to let your immediate impression of the candidate colour the way you describe the job. If your impression is unfavourable, you may emphasise the drawbacks in the job, and vice versa. Any candidate who accepts the job, and then feels they were talked into it, or misled during their interview, will only cause you problems in the long run.

Invite questions

The applicant for a job is probably making a larger commitment than the organisation taking them on. It will mean more change in their life than it will for the life of the organisation. This means that applicants should have every chance to ask any questions.

A good approach to this stage is briefly to describe the job, and then to offer an open question that allows them to choose the direction of the conversation: '... so, that is the basic role. What part of the job would you like to know more about?'

Reflect on the candidates' questions

The type of questions the candidates ask will reveal something about themselves.

- Have they prepared for this interview?
- Have they done some basic research on your organisation?
- What interests them most about the job (salary, holiday entitlement or the type of work)?
- Are they interested in the job or in a career?
- Have they asked about further training and other future opportunities?
- Do they have the confidence to ask searching questions, or are they reticent?

Closing

When time is up, or the interview has run its course, you need to close it down while leaving the candidates with the feeling that they have had a fair hearing and a chance to 'sell themselves'.

- Thank the candidate
- Explain to them what the next stage will be
- If expenses are payable, check that they know what to do about them
- Clarify when they will hear from you one way or another.

Taking notes
If you are interviewing more than one person it will be almost essential to take notes – few people have perfect memories! When taking notes:

- Mention it to the candidate in a matter-of-fact way. Point out that you want to make sure you get the facts right.
- Avoid making notes immediately after the candidate has made a mistake or been unable to answer a question (ask an easy follow-up question and then take a note).
- Remember that in the unlikely event of a complaint your notes could be subpoenaed by a tribunal.

After the interview
Review your notes and add any details that you think are relevant. Ask yourself if you have at least one candidate who could do the job well, and meets all the essential criteria in your personal profile. If there is more than one suitable candidate, ask yourself who would bring the most added value to the job. If none is outstanding, ask yourself: will the best of what you have got do, or should you start again? (Remember your long-term organisation plan.)

Write to all the candidates, and do anything else that you undertook to do during the interview. Keep your notes, and review them in the light of the successful applicant's first year's work. This can be a valuable check on your selection process and the interview in particular.

Panel interviews

Many large organisations use panel interviews. Panels are usually three or four people, each with a particular responsibility such as knowledge of the job, the technical expert, personnel policies, training and so forth.

Advantages
The advantages of panel interviews include:

- Emphasising the importance of the selection task; all the members should prepare carefully for their role.
- Panel members can focus on their own responsibility, bringing specialist knowledge to the interview.
- Panel members can correct each other if someone mishears the candidate.
- The chair of the panel can control the timing and pace of the interview.
- Responsibility for the selection process is shared by a team who are all working from the same information.

Disadvantages
Panel interviews have their drawbacks too.

- Organisations used to committee-based decision-making can use the panel interview to dilute responsibility for decisions, ending up with 'compromise' selections.
- Panels are more expensive and difficult to organise than one-to-one interviews. If one member is late the whole process is delayed.
- Applicants are less likely to feel at ease when they are outnumbered. If all the interviewers face the candidate the interview may feel more like an inquisition.
- Chairing a panel is not easy. Poor chairing skills may mean an unbalanced interview, or worse, one that runs out of time.
- Panel members may be reticent about speaking their minds in front of colleagues, or might attempt to impress their colleagues at the expense of the purpose of the interview.

Serial interviews

If several people need to see the candidate, a good arrangement is to organise a series of one-to-one interviews. Each interviewer will have to take careful and consistent notes, but the subsequent selection will be based on a wide range of information.

CHAPTER 3
Induction

What is induction?

Some weeks can pass between the selection interview and the offer and acceptance of a job; the difficulties, anxieties and potential embarrassments may soon be forgotten. When the successful applicant reports for work, the next interview you have to manage will be the induction interview.

As with any other interview, preparation starts with defining the aim. Make a note of the aim for an induction interview you may be planning. There are two things to consider. First, the aim of most induction interviews is to help the recruit become as productive as possible as soon as possible. Secondly, remember that the recruit will have needs and concerns that must be met as well. Review your aim to cover both your (or the organisation's) needs *and* those of the recruit. If your aim is broad, it may take several interviews to cover all the ground. The new recruit will have to take in a lot of information, which is best delivered in small doses if you want to avoid giving them mental indigestion.

The induction interview is only part of the overall induction process, which may include site tours, courses and department visits; but it is the part that provides the foundation of future relationships between you as the boss and your employee. The more complex or responsible the job of the recruit, the more time spent on careful induction will pay for itself. The induction interview needs to be planned so that the style of the interview matches its main purpose. If you spend an hour explaining that staff involvement is welcomed, but the new recruit hardly gets a word in, ask yourself what message are they really receiving.

Aim
To help the new recruit to:

- clarify their role in the organisation
- learn fast and start being a useful member of the team
- ask anything they feel they need to know.

Planning
- What is your aim?
- What will they want to know or do?
- If you don't know this, how will you find out?
- Can you assess their mood or attitude?
- Is there anything you need to do or say to correct this (if required)?
- Will this be a single event or the start of a series of meetings?
- Do you want simply to inform your interviewee or to generate a two-way process?

Preparation
- Plan the whole of the recruit's first day (if possible) to set the context of your interview.
- Investigate your employee as far as possible, check with previous interviewers, documentation from selection and correspondence etc.
- Check you have all the paperwork, brochures and job description details you need.
- Plan the locations and timings for the day: the interview, site tour and department visits.
- Double-check that people you need to visit are still available.
- Make sure your own interview will be uninterrupted.
- Allow time for the employee to meet other staff.

Structure
- Congratulate and welcome the employee.
- Ask if there are any problems.
- Explain the purpose and programme for the day.
- Check if they have any enquiries.
- Adjust your interview agenda if needed.
- Explain the outline of the job, and how it fits in with other jobs.
- Explain how job progress will be measured or assessed.
- Provide back-up information about the job.
- Introduce the people the employee will meet or need to work with.
- Explain the amenities at work.
- Clarify any local customs, work hours, leave arrangements and so on.
- Agree on any action points and sum up.
- Any further questions?

Follow-up
- Does the employee seem contented?
- Are they able to explain their needs?
- Is the work going well?
- Are initial targets being met?
- Are there any 'settling down' problems?
- Did the interview suggest that the employee needed any special guidance or help?
- Was it in fact needed, and was it provided?
- Plan the follow-up interviews.

Case study
David's induction

A typical induction programme for a middle-grade job in an organisation might include:

Day 1
1. Welcome, brief introduction to other staff.
2. Show David his place of work, desk and the resources he

will use (include essential safety rules if necessary), followed by a tour of his department or section.
3. Explanation of the main work of the section, and its context within the mission and purpose of the whole organisation.
4. Personal interview to cover:

- Any questions he has
- Overview of main work of the section
- Contractual details: hours of work, company car, annual leave, etc
- Visit staff rooms, toilets, canteen, etc
- Introduction to a colleague to take him to lunch
- Afternoon spent becoming familiar with usual work details, papers, forms, procedures and so on.

Day 2
1. Interview David to check details from Day 1 and answer any queries.
2. Further explanation of his work, range of responsibilities and limits to his authority.
3. Allow him to work through some typical work 'cases' or examples as relevant.
4. Arrange meetings to introduce his colleagues or staff, and allow him to orient himself.
5. Afternoon spent reviewing work details, and how he will relate to his main contacts and with other departments.

Day 3
Hold a follow-up interview with David's immediate manager to review his first two days and agree further meetings as required.

The rest of the first week
David should:

- Meet personnel to confirm details of his pay and pension, etc.
- Meet the safety officer, or attend a safety course as appropriate

- Meet representatives from other departments he will have to work with, so he has a 'network' of contacts as soon as possible.

CHAPTER 4
Coaching

The manager as coach

There are few jobs where the new employee will not need some form of explanation or training if they are to meet your standards. A training course will meet some of the basic needs, but there is no substitute for 'private tuition' by you as the manager. Your staff work for you, you are responsible for their targets, and so are also responsible for ensuring that they have the knowledge and skills needed for good job performance.

Management coaching is not often thought of as an 'interview', but it fulfils the definition very well. Coaching must have a clear training aim or objective, and is best used for aspects of the job where the employee needs to be creative, or use their initiative. Examples include handling difficult customers or making fine judgements about quality. This means the aim will be achieved through discussion as much as by instruction. More routine parts of the job could be learnt from manuals or instructor-centred courses. In complex jobs, management coaching is necessary for developing staff. In NVQ terms this would mean Level 3 and above.

Coaching is a form of training. This means that three aspects of the interview become very important.

1. A clear aim is essential. Clarify exactly what you expect the employee to be able *to do* after the interview.

2. Involve them in the interview. Few people learn much by being lectured at even when the lecture is for them alone.
3. Check afterwards whether your explanation was effective and that the trainee has been able to apply the learning successfully at work.

Aim
To make sure your employee learns the skills or attitudes they need for their job.

Planning
- Define exactly what you want your employee to be able to do, or do better.
- Write this out in terms of the ability or competence they will need. Clarify what support, manuals or tools they will have and any special conditions they may have to work under.
- Check on their existing ability.
- Break down into small steps the task they need to perform.
- Decide how you will actively involve them in the learning.
- Plan how you will check that they have grasped the practical skills and any decision-making or thinking that goes with it.
- Constantly bear in mind the learning from their point of view.
- Allow more time than you think will be needed.

Preparation
- Start with an overview, and 'zoom in' to the detail.
- Have plenty of practical examples and finished items.
- Double-check that any aids, PC software or other equipment is available and in working order.
- Remember that the more you know about the task, the easier it is to overlook the obvious!

Structure
- Explain the purpose of the session. Ask about previous experience.

- Clarify the exact objective of the coaching.
- Explain why they need to achieve the objective.
- Demonstrate the skill or task at normal speed.
- Demonstrate in small stages at slow speed, asking your employee to copy what you do.
- Explain and quiz them about any thinking that needs to go with the task.
- Check their understanding at each step.
- Ask them to do it for themselves, explaining what they do as they go.
- Focus on quality, not speed.

Follow-up
- Make sure your employee has plenty of opportunity to practise the task.
- Arrange a follow-up interview to check for speed as well as quality of work.
- Check that the coaching has helped them in their job.
- If further coaching is needed, re-analyse the task and start planning again.

Case study
Coaching Colin

Review this transcription of part of an instruction interview, and make notes on how you would advise the coach to improve the effectiveness of the coaching interview style.

Coach: Right, here you are then, this is a multimeter, you will need to know about these.

Colin: Yes I've used something like that before.

Coach: Oh good, then this should be simple enough then. Right. You always set it to 2000V first, see, for safety, and then make sure that you hold the probes like this. Now touch each contact in turn and see what the reading is on this scale here.

Colin: Which scale? There seem to be several.

Coach: The high volts one, of course. Then if the reading is below, say, 200, you can switch to a lower scale for a better reading. See?

Colin: Oh, er, well yes.

Here the coach has waded straight into the subject, and obviously knows a lot about the meter, but:

- Has not checked Colin's previous experience, and even ignored the hint that he had 'used something like that before'
- Is doing all the talking, and not asking any checking questions
- Is not involving Colin at all – the coach is probably still holding the instrument, and the hapless Colin has not yet laid hands on it
- Has not explained the different scales on the instrument, and uses vague phrases such as 'for safety' or 'better reading'. What are the dangers and what makes the reading better?

This second coach knows more about coaching, and starts by finding out how much Colin knows, and then builds on that:

Coach: Right then, you will need to use a digital meter on this next job, it can save you hours of investigation work if you can use this well. Here, take hold of this. Have you used one before?

Colin: Yes, but it was a multimeter type.

Coach: Good, this is similar, but more sensitive, so it is easier to be more accurate. What do you know about the scales?

Colin: Well I was told always start with the high range and work down, but no one ever explained why.

Coach: You're quite right. Click it round to the high range, that's it, good; now the reason is a question of safety...

Colin is actively involved straight away ('here, take hold of this') and the coach can build on existing knowledge because

Colin is answering questions. The coach explains the benefit of learning the task ('this can save you...') and encourages Colin to make verbal and practical responses.

CHAPTER 5
Grievance

Being constructive about grievances

Most managers do not like dealing with a grievance. You may probably also have a defensive emotional reaction when criticism is laid at your door. Sensitive handling of a grievance, however, can be a valuable source of feedback about your department, and being curt or seeming to ignore it will usually do more harm than good.

Overcome your instinct, and respond to a grievance rather than just react to it. You will not always have much chance to plan a grievance interview, so some general points have to be thought out in advance that you can apply at short notice.

The actual complaint may not always be the real trouble, so take care to allow people to 'let off steam', feel they are being taken seriously, and then find out what the real grievance is. Complaints about the canteen, for example, are almost traditional, but are often a mask for a basic dissatisfaction that is best aired and dealt with. Strikes about money or other measurable rewards occur less because of low wages than because of the low status they symbolise.

Grievances are one of a range of interviews that can become quite heated. In all of these apply the basic NAFOF principle:

Never Assume, Find Out First.

Finally, while it is good management to be sympathetic, and pay attention to people's needs for personal or emotional support at work, you may sometimes need to remind staff that an individual tail cannot be allowed to wag the organisational dog.

Aim
- To offer a hearing and improve morale.
- To emphasise that management is always open to reasonable comments.
- If it is justified, to resolve the grievance.

Planning
- Take the approach seriously, possibly thanking the employee for bringing it up.
- Even if the complaint is manifestly false, remember that it has been presented for a reason.
- Avoid taking sides or making a judgement until you have all the facts.
- Be sympathetic, but be prepared to break off the interview until you have the facts.
- The best way to calm people is to listen to them, and plan some action. Counter-criticism is usually counter-productive.
- Some grievances are actually caused by the lack of skill (including social skills) of the complainant; many grievance interviews need a follow-up counselling interview.

Preparation
- If you are given notice of the interview, investigate beforehand to get the facts.
- Prepare to listen; respond, don't just react.
- Ensure privacy; if you walk into a fracas, separate the parties and see them separately.
- Be prepared to accept nothing in writing until a day has gone by; many rows will cool below the action threshold by then.

Structure
- Welcome and listen to the grievance.
- Restate it in your own words.
- Let the other person blow off steam if needed, but not beyond what is reasonable behaviour at work.
- Beware of taking sides; clarify your role and the organisation's policy if needed.
- Listen and restate until you are both in reasonable agreement about what the problem really is.
- Give your interpretation of the facts if that seems useful.
- If necessary, get agreement to another interview when you have got the facts, the third party's version, or whatever else you need to find out.
- If a delay is inevitable, remind the employee that meanwhile you expect business as usual.
- Say what you intend to do (without limiting your ability to act if something unexpected turns up).
- Explain the reasons for your interpretation and actions.
- Check that the employee is satisfied with your decisions.
- End on an appreciative and possibly sympathetic note.

Follow-up
- Follow up any action you promised.
- Check that the matter is resolved, and no further complication has arisen.
- Check on work standards and performance.
- Reflect on any action you may need to take to ensure that the problem does not occur again.

Case study
Problems in a legal office

In a large law firm, all photocopying over 20 pages was left for the reprographics technician, usually giving 24 hours' notice. One young lawyer, Nigel, often needed copies at less notice for his corporate clients but could not always get them. After one particularly frustrating day he finally complained to his boss that Moira, the technician, was dilatory and unhelpful to him. Moira had a good reputation, so the boss thanked Nigel, said he would look into it, and agreed a meeting for the next day.

He found that on one occasion Moira had indeed not met her usual 'next day' target, but she had been in the middle of a print run of brochures. She had also not been inclined to put herself out for someone whom she described as abrupt and discourteous. The boss explained the facts to Nigel, and agreed he was technically correct in his complaint, but suggested that presumably the outcome he really wanted was a better service from Moira. He asked Nigel to describe the events from Moira's point of view.

The result was that if Nigel improved his work planning most of his copying was not as urgent as he made out. When short notice was inevitable, he usually knew in advance, although the papers were only ready at the last minute. Nigel agreed that he could give Moira more notice of such jobs, and she could then plan for them. A potential complaint was turned into an improvement in work style and better communication between employees.

CHAPTER 6
Counselling

When to counsel

A lot of your contact with your staff involves giving them instructions and resolving problems. Some problems, however, are not amenable to stronger or clearer instructions. The counselling interview can resolve conflicts that other approaches don't seem to help.

First spend a moment listing the sorts of problems that you have to deal with, where simply giving more instructions does not help. Think of those cases where you might be tempted to say something like 'Pull yourself together' or 'Come on, just get on with it', but your better judgement knows that such advice rarely makes much difference.

The problems you have listed, among others, probably include a combination of the following two types:

1. Problems that people bring to work with them from home, whose burden affects their work standards. A member of staff facing a divorce, or whose partner or children are in trouble with the law, may be unlikely to take much care with their work.
2. Problems that are not too serious in themselves, but that affect other people, and the disruption they cause, are the real nuisance for you as a manager. Someone who is constantly complaining, or who chatters cheerfully when

others are trying to concentrate, will affect the morale and output of everyone, while they may appear to be unaware of it themselves.

How counselling works

Probably neither the domestic nor the behavioural problems will be resolved by encouragement ('It's not that bad', 'Come on, you'll get over it') or by giving advice ('If I were you ... ', 'What you need to do is ... '). The best approach is to prepare a counselling interview, and this is where you have to manage by relinquishing your role as a manager. You are in charge of the interview, but you are *not* responsible for solving the problem.

Counselling is a process whereby one person helps another to solve the problem for themselves. You may have noticed that when you have a personal problem the advice others so freely give is often irrelevant, even useless, and it is based on their experience rather than yours. In counselling you do not give instructions, or offer advice based on your experience: you give the other person a chance to think it through, and decide how best to help themselves. The counsellor provides the opportunity for thought, but the client does the deciding.

This approach can be successful even where someone's actions are causing a problem for you (such as the chatterbox above), because if you could have resolved it by simply asking them to be more considerate you would have done so. Since, presumably, that would not have worked, no amount of telling them would work either. An inconsiderate person has to come to their own conclusion about the effects of their behaviour, and then resolve to change. Little else will have much effect. For example, try telling a smoker to give up; they might agree that they should, but they are unlikely to do so until they really want to for themselves.

By the nature of the interview, your interviewee (or client) is largely in charge of the content of a counselling interview. As the counsellor you are responsible for the style, atmosphere, and most of the structure. This is hard to plan for. Planning is more a matter of seeing the benefit of adopting a reflective attitude, and accepting that giving advice rarely works.

In counselling interviews you:

- need to be patient and mainly listen
- will use a lot of reflective and summarising questions
- use restating to check that you have understood their point of view
- may have quite long pauses while the other person thinks
- should suppress the urge to 'advise'
- may use questions to open up possible options
- need to control the structure and progress of the interview to avoid a self-pity session
- have to accept that they may choose a plan of action that you think is less than the best in the circumstances.

Occasionally counselling may involve your providing some impartial information to help the other person to make their decision, but beware of being drawn into helping to resolve the problem itself. For example:

Counsellor: Look, shall I give the housing office a call and see if the flat can be put into your sole name? I think that would be a good idea.

Here the counsellor is being drawn into taking responsibility for solving the problem, taking initiative away from the client, and may be imposing their own 'solution'.

Counsellor: Would it help if I found the telephone number of the Council Housing Office for you?

This is a useful offer to provide information and thereby open a possible course of action for the client to consider, without 'advising'.

If you become involved in resolving the problem you may encourage your client to depend on you for more help.

Fostering such dependence may lead to a poor working relationship. Furthermore, if your suggestion does not work, your client may well blame you, and you may get drawn further into the mire.

Aim
To help someone else to think through their problem and decide on a course of action.

Planning
The counselling interview is where you act as a counsellor to your client and:

- Listen to their views no matter how strange they seem to you
- Help them to feel they are being taken seriously
- Give them the time to express themselves
- Help them to clarify the problem
- Let them feel that no judgements are being made about them
- Help them to weigh up possible courses of action.

If they feel it is useful, you can help to plan some action *they* can take to make progress.

Preparation
- Keep an open eye for changes in behaviour or attitude that may signify problems that need to be dealt with.
- Ensure strict privacy, including (if possible) giving the impression that the interview never took place.
- Avoid taking sides.
- Beware of being drawn into the problem itself.
- Remember that you are still the manager, even though you take a back seat during the interview.

Structure
- Clarify your role and purpose.
- Explain why you have invited the discussion.

- Give any relevant facts or observations you have.
- Ensure confidentiality (see below for the one exception to this).
- Explain the structure of the interview.
- Invite them to explain themselves.
- Ensure you have understood; check the facts.
- Invite them to list the possible options.
- Encourage them to choose the best one.
- Encourage them to plan their first step.
- Make sure they know they can meet you again.

Follow-up
There are two outcomes to a counselling session depending on the type of problem.

1. For personal problems:
   - Say and do nothing
   - Ensure that they know you are available for another discussion if they want one. If you have been able to help them, they will return if they want more help. If they feel you have not been of much help, which they may or may not admit, inviting them for follow-up discussion would be pointless.
2. For problems that behaviour was causing to you as a manager:
   - Check that work standards are back to normal
   - Make sure that complaints and other difficulties have been resolved
   - Limit your follow-up strictly to your managerial rather than counselling role.

Two outcomes with special dangers

Some interviews start innocently enough, and then, following an assurance of confidentiality, the employee admits that they have actually committed a serious offence. Can you now break your confidentiality and turn the interview into a disciplinary one? You need to bear in mind that the interview is at work, and you both know that you are still the manager. An effective approach is to point out that you cannot ignore what you have just heard, and ask the employee what should be done next. Few people mind a fair outcome, what they resent is arbitrary justice. They will often agree that the offence has to be dealt with, even if it includes some form of penalty, especially if you give them credit for having come to talk to you in the first place.

The second outcome that can be difficult is when it becomes clear that the employee has a serious personal problem, and you feel you are being drawn into a supporting role that exceeds your job as a manager. Again, remember that this interview is at work, and you can legitimately explain that the conversation is getting beyond your responsibility. Guide your employee to thinking about where they could go for more professional or qualified help. Most doctors' surgeries have a list of a wide range of support groups for people with medical or social problems. The Samaritans, Relate and the Citizens' Advice Bureau all offer trained help.

As a manager your role includes supporting and training your staff, but this presupposes that they are mentally and socially fit to carry out their job. If you feel a counselling interview is getting you slightly out of your depth, agree a break, and seek advice from your own manager or from your personnel office.

Case study
A new recruit unsettles the team

Jackie, the manager of a telesales team, received a complaint from one staff member that a recent recruit was upsetting the others. When Joan joined them they had been working well together for over two years, and the others were becoming reluctant to share their shifts with her. Jackie carefully asked why this was. She discovered that Joan had the habit of chatting about quite personal matters, and the others found this uncomfortable. They were starting to shun Joan, who only seemed to get even more personal. Jackie did nothing until she could be seen to have overheard one such conversation.

Over coffee at the end of one shift, she congratulated Joan on the standard of her work, and asked how she got on with the others. 'Funny you mention that,' was the reply, 'I've made a real effort to get on with them, but they just don't seem to respond.'

'Yes, you do come over as a very open person,' replied Jackie, 'I couldn't help overhearing you telling Julie about your daughter's diet fad ....'

Avoiding the temptation to give advice, Jackie steered the conversation to asking Joan how she thought the existing team would react to such frankness in her first week.

'You think I am trying too hard then?' asked the recruit.

'Well,' answered Jackie, 'I think only you can really judge that, but it does seem to explain what you were saying. What do you think might be a better approach ...?'

CHAPTER 7
The Correction Interview

To distinguish correction from reprimand

There is a difference between a correction interview and a reprimand interview, so you will need to plan and prepare for them differently. To deserve a reprimand (and possibly incur a penalty), your employee must be blameworthy. If they have done something wrong, but it is not their fault, they only deserve a correction.

The person who has made the error tends to confuse these two interviews. If it was not their fault (for example, the mistake was due to poor training, or genuinely unforeseeable circumstances), and it seems to them the criticism is unjustified, they may be uncooperative, argue their side fiercely or nurse a grudge, depending on their temperament. None of these makes for a productive interview.

On the other hand, someone who knows they are at fault has a vested interest in seeing it interpreted as a mere correction. They may be evasive or seek to blame others. Your task is to clarify what the interview really is, and plan it accordingly.

Aim
- To improve work standards or performance.
- To prevent repetition of the error.
- To protect others from carelessness or even danger.

Planning
Use correction rather than reprimand for:

- trivial errors
- first offences that don't have serious consequences
- people in a training period
- people in a new job, or using new procedures.

Distinguish between 'new errors' (such as teething problems with a new procedure) and errors in an existing and established method of work. In the case of a new error clarify exactly how you want them to change. Think of correction as a form of training.

Preparation
- Get the facts; you will need to distinguish between deliberate and unwitting errors. You may find that you were partly at fault. If so, admit it without dwelling on it.
- Arrange the interview as soon as possible after the error.
- In the case of a new error ensure that others are briefed too.
- Take action outside the interview to avoid repetition of the error.

Structure
- Point out the effects of the error.
- State the facts as you know them.
- Ask the employee if it is clear that it is an error.
- Clarify that no blame is attached.
- Depending on the nature of the error, either ask the employee for ideas on how the error might be avoided, or demonstrate the correct method or procedure.
- Ask them to explain the method back to you to check their understanding.
- Thank them, and ensure they know to come back to you if they have any doubts.

Follow-up
- Check that the mistake is not made again.

- If it is, consider reprimanding.
- If it is not, congratulate.
- Give the employee a chance to ask any further questions that they may have thought of since the interview.

Case study
The new typist

Dora, an architect, asked central personnel for a replacement typist, and she was sent Lynda, a typist redeployed from another department. Lynda's standards were poor, and Dora decided to approach her tactfully, show her examples of good and bad letters and ask her to suggest how she could improve. Lynda had little to say and Dora ended up simply giving clear instructions how she wanted her letters to be set out. She later overheard another secretary report Lynda as saying 'Oh, isn't she sarcastic? "How do you think it should be done?" Why doesn't she just say?'. Dora realised that she had misjudged Lynda's approach to her work — an attempt at tact had been badly misinterpreted and Dora had not adequately explained things in the first place. Lynda's attitude was not insolent, she was simply the type of person who preferred to be just told what to do.

CHAPTER 8
The Reprimand Interview

All part of management

The aims of a reprimand interview are the same as those for a
correction. Your main task as a manager is to see that work
progresses smoothly, so the objective here is neither to punish
the wrongdoer (although there may be a penalty to pay), nor
is it to pass moral judgement. The outcome is to prevent a
recurrence of the error.

A reprimand interview is sometimes called a disciplinary
interview. The word 'discipline' comes from 'disciple', or
'follower'. Your aim is to ensure that people follow what is
expected of them within the context of their employment.

As noted in Chapter 7, only people who are clearly at fault
deserve a reprimand as opposed to a correction. If they sense
that they will have a penalty to pay for their actions, they may
try to evade the blame or attempt to foist it on another party.
Always bear in mind that managers are as capable of errors as
other staff, and while you may have investigated carefully,
there is always the possibility that you start the interview with
the wrong, or incomplete, facts of the matter.

The reprimand is one of the hardest tasks you have to face
as a manager. Put simply: you cannot be effective and always
popular, and this interview can strain the loyalty between you
and the people who work for you. However, it is part of a
manager's job: a manager who cannot reprimand (where it is

justified) is as bad as one who cannot lead or give instructions. Loyalty to your boss, an organisation, must sometimes outweigh other feelings. In fact, managers who reprimand fairly are usually more respected by their staff than those who cannot.

Reprimands are charged with emotion; both parties may have strong feelings about the subject. Here you have to be careful to avoid emotive language or unjustified criticism. This interview is not a planned argument, but a realistic statement of disagreeable facts. If you have *any* doubt about your organisation's policy on verbal warnings and disciplinary matters, take advice. More workplace trouble is caused by precipitate action by managers than by almost any other cause.

Aim
- To improve work standards or performance.
- To prevent repetition of the error.
- To protect others from carelessness or even danger.

Planning
- Check your organisation's policy on dealing with first offences, verbal warnings, etc.
- Investigate and get the facts; be sure of your ground.
- If necessary, postpone the interview until you have adequate facts.
- Research the individual's record.
- Plan your approach in relation to the individual concerned.

Preparation
- Reprimand in private − even those presumed guilty are allowed their dignity.
- Give the employee notice of the time and place.
- For a serious offence, remind them they may be accompanied by a representative. You may wish for a member of personnel staff to attend too.
- Bear in mind you may be wrong!

Structure
- Get straight to the point and state the facts as you know them.
- Ask the employee for their version of events.
- Get agreement of the facts; be exact.
- Avoid any arguments; focus on facts and events, not personalities.
- Give your interpretation.
- If there is doubt, postpone the interview until you have complete information.
- Check the employee's understanding of the consequences of their actions, both to their colleagues (the reasons behind the rules), and to themselves (any sanctions or penalty).
- Explain how they can improve, and show your confidence that they can do so.

Follow-up
- For a serious error, summarise the interview in writing.
- See that the error does not recur.
- Do not show antagonism.
- Keep an eye on work attitudes.
- Ensure 'business as usual'.

Case study
Unauthorised absence

Phil, the personnel manager of a retail chain, was surprised to find one of his field staff, Diane, had to call him back when he phoned the store she should have been working in. On checking up, he discovered that Diane had gone home, and had asked the store staff to cover for her. Diane was normally a reliable person, and this deception was out of character, but it had clearly taken place.

Phil asked her to come to head office to meet him. He felt this would set a suitably formal tone for their meeting. She did not dispute the facts, and simply said, 'Well, I'll take the punishment'. Phil felt this was not a suitable attitude for a trusted field-based professional, and used open questions, pauses and encouragement to get a better explanation. It turned out that Diane had a serious problem at home, and taken a day off to deal with it. She said she did not think Phil would have understood, but now saw differently.

The outcome of this sensitive interviewing was a day's lost leave, close reporting for a month, and a better boss–subordinate relationship, instead of a written warning on the file of a good member of staff.

CHAPTER 9
The Appraisal Interview

Talking about progress

Whenever a boss and subordinate meet, just the two of them, to discuss the subordinate's progress, it is an appraisal interview. This is the most difficult interview to conduct, as it calls for all the skills needed for other types of interview. Appraisals are often made up of different strands, serving different purposes, and the main skill in conducting them is to recognise the purpose of each strand, and to deal with them separately.

An annual appraisal interview is a more formal version of the regular short-term appraisals that you should be giving to your staff during the year. It is more formal because the result is usually recorded for the use of both parties.

As with all interviews, if either side has no clear idea of the purpose, the interview can degenerate into a pointless embarrassment. This is particularly true of the appraisal interview, as subordinates will tend to feel they are being judged, and the manager may be nervous about the whole process of being put on record.

The main aim of an appraisal interview is to help subordinates. However, if the person being appraised feels that the process is something to be endured, or an examination that they must pass to obtain a salary rise, then the interview will be an unproductive and guarded exchange rather than an open process that is helpful to both sides.

What can the appraisal interview achieve?

The aims of an appraisal interview can be wide, and may include:

- To improve an individual's performance by knowledge of results
- To reconcile the ambitions of the employee with the employer's business objectives
- To improve communication between boss and subordinate
- To help an individual to see and overcome failings, and prevent recurrence of previous difficulties
- To help the subordinate to develop any useful talents
- To give recognition for good work
- To plan future work and set targets or objectives
- To help the manager to see and overcome any managerial or organisational failings.

Why is it difficult?

The word 'appraise' is defined as 'to estimate the amount, or worth of'. Unfortunately, 'appraisal' implies to many employees that the main point of this process is to judge them in an unproductive way. It is usually better to point out in your opening remarks that the emphasis in appraisal should be on 'praise'. Start by giving fair and due recognition for all the good work that has been done since the last appraisal interview. This may be a twist of the true meaning of the word, but it is a more productive and motivating introduction to the interview.

People do not like to be 'judged' like second-hand cars, and many managers do not relish the role of assessor. This is particularly true of interviews that are clearly linked to annual salary reviews. Modern motivation studies all point to the fact that (given an adequate minimum salary) most people work harder for intangible rewards such as recognition and a sense of achievement. If your appraisal interviews are to be constructive and productive for both parties then you should prepare them to satisfy the wants and needs of both you and your subordinate. Your respective wants and needs may not always be the same thing.

The subordinate may *want*:

- Praise
- Recognition
- The opportunity to ask for more interesting work
- The chance to ask for a rise or promotion
- A platform to air their grievances about you or the organisation
- Unconditional forgiveness of past errors.

Whereas they may *need*:

- Some helpful feedback on their performance
- A more realistic view of their abilities or ambitions
- Closer targets and objectives to work towards
- The realisation that opportunities to improve come from constructive criticism.

You may *want*:

- The chance to say exactly what you feel about the subordinate
- An excuse for giving them less interesting work, or refusing promotion
- An opportunity to criticise their work in a way that does not arise from daily contact.

Whereas you too may *need*:

- Some honest feedback on your performance
- A chance to find out how you are seen by the subordinate (or other staff)
- Constructive comments on how you can help staff to perform better.

There are many other difficulties:

- Boss and subordinate are nervous or anxious about changing their previous relationship.
- Annual appraisal is a solemn occasion; how can you be on easy terms with a subordinate one day, and then give bad news about promotion the next?
- Any unresolved or outstanding grievance smouldering between the two parties can come to the surface during the interview, offending both but without resolving the conflict.
- Many people have difficulty in being open about serious or important things without embarrassment. They may even avoid some topics simply because of this.
- If the appraisal is a matter of a one-way evaluation, the result is likely to be subjective. The 'halo effect' often seen in selection interviews can apply here too.
- Some subordinates may be quick-witted at interviews, and bosses may be uncomfortable about this.
- The harsh truth may simply be depressing. To tell someone that their hopes of advancement are groundless may merely cause their performance to suffer rather than to improve.

Cooperative annual appraisals

Effective appraisal interviews have to be cooperative ventures between managers and subordinates. This will mean that each needs to be open to constructive comment by the other, and to approach the interview as an opportunity to learn and improve rather than being defensive. In planning your appraisal interviews start by looking at the topics from the other point of view. Ask yourself what they will want from this interview. The annual appraisal is a time for the manager to stop giving rulings and orders, and to allow subordinates to feel that they have an opportunity to give advice, to be listened to, and to commit themselves to their development strategy and their work for the coming year.

As in the counselling interview, you do not have to agree to everything you hear, but you need to accept that the most effective appraisal is a two-way process. If you cannot come to an agreement during an appraisal it is usually better to 'agree to disagree' and move on. Later a senior manager can be the judge of the matter by hearing both sides of the argument.

Peer and subordinate appraisal

This is an increasingly used variation of appraisals. The interviewee's colleagues and subordinates are invited to comment on each other's performance (sometimes using a standard form) and these comments are on the table during the appraisal. This may seem to invite anonymous and cynical remarks, but where it is used openly it can provide many helpful pointers.

Should appraisal interviews be linked to salary increases?

No. There are many arguments for and against direct linkage between the output of appraisal interviews and increases in remuneration, salary, company car or other perks, but on balance they are best kept apart. Remember that the main aim of an appraisal interview is to help the subordinate to improve their work. It is clearly helpful for both boss and subordinate to know what is required to earn more money or to receive other rewards, and it can be useful to plan a meeting to discuss and agree these factors. However, if subordinates sense that they have to pass muster in some way in their appraisal interview, that interview is unlikely to be an open and productive discussion. The appraisees will be clearly trying to show themselves in their best light, while the boss may be guarded and unable to give staff the assurances that they would like.

If appraisal interviews are to help subordinates to develop, by helping them to see their shortcomings and commit themselves to improvement, you will need to create an atmosphere of openness and mutual trust. Salary and other rewards are issues that should be kept out of a genuine appraisal interview.

Meetings to discuss salaries

Organisations that do not use appraisal interviews to discuss salaries (because the topic often dominates the interview) arrange quite separate meetings, often called staff planning meetings or salary reviews. The agenda is clear, and the atmosphere is one of cooperative negotiation. The manager should be armed with hard information about pay policies, and possible rises or other rewards, and the subordinates know that to earn them they will have to accept the targets or other conditions. Trust and constructive criticism do not come into it. Consider this exchange:

Manager: So if you reach your sales figures you could be in for a promotion.

Subordinate: Could you confirm that in a memo for me?

Manager: Why? Don't you trust me?

Subordinate: It's not a matter of trust, I'm happy to accept the challenge, but in a year's time either of us could have moved, and memories are not perfect. I see this as an agreement, and if it is written down we both know where we stand.

Manager: Well put like that I see what you mean, but it will also imply that if you don't reach the standard — then no promotion.

Subordinate: That's fair enough. As I said, it's an agreement and there are always two sides.

Short-term and long-term appraisals

We need to distinguish between these two forms of appraisal interview. As a manager you should be giving continual feedback to your staff on their performance, and what they need to do to stay on target. Some managers organise weekly or monthly meetings on work progress. During such appraisal meetings the managers may receive helpful comments on what they could do to improve the progress of work. These meetings are informal, and they are not usually recorded in any detail. An annual appraisal interview is simply a once-a-year occasion to summarise formally all the appraisals during the year and record what is agreed for the next year. Annual appraisals should not contain any great surprises for either side.

Appraisal forms

Many companies and public sector organisations have official forms to be completed during an annual appraisal. These often list various job attributes and invite the manager to rate the subordinate from 'needs improvement' to 'above standard'. Appraisers are usually asked to add a comment if they have marked either extreme of the scale. Some departments of the civil service still have a complex form using numbers, and if the total is less than 100, the interviewee is not considered for promotion. Such documents are likely to have a stultifying effect on the degree of openness during the interview.

Appraisal forms can be useful because they:

- Are a record of the meeting
- Are an agreement by both sides of what was discussed
- Show trends over the years of an individual's career
- Show trends of one manager's assessment compared with others
- Provide a reference document for each party during the next twelve months
- Establish some consistency if either party moves before the next appraisal
- Record agreed targets for the coming year
- Enable compilation of company-wide training needs.

The drawback of forms is that they:

- Can limit the interview topics to the list on the form
- Tend to look back rather than forward
- Risk focusing the interview on evaluation rather than on improvement
- Increase the likelihood that subordinates will feel the need to defend themselves

● Invite 'middle of the road' evaluation.

By reducing appraisal to quantitive box-ticking the general influence of such forms is to focus on the evaluation of the past by the manager. The subordinate will become defensive to counter what is seen as critical measurement. A useful and more constructive approach to forms is when both you and your subordinate use them as a checklist before the interview in an open reporting system.

Open or confidential reporting?

The general trend in management is to have open reporting appraisals, where the interviewees are given notice of the interview, and asked to prepare for it by:

● Reviewing the targets agreed in the previous year
● Assessing their own performance over the past year
● Drafting their own targets for the coming year.

The appraisal form can be a useful checklist. The manager will do the same, and the resulting interview is mainly based on discussion, comparing notes, and agreeing the final assessment on the form.

Three important benefits arise from this approach.

1. Managers consistently report that self-assessment by subordinates results in them being more critical of themselves than many managers would dare to be. This allows the manager to be more generous in the interview.
2. Targets and objectives for the coming year are more likely to be reached if they have been discussed, negotiated and agreed, rather than simply imposed.
3. Discussions on training needs arise from an agreement of the skills that need to be developed or brought up to standard, and self-assessment results in a more constructive approach to training. (Trainers frequently report that some course delegates simply announce that they 'have been

sent' when asked what they want to get out of the course. Such human parcels are probably wasting their time compared with those who know exactly what benefits they are expecting.)

Training

Appraisal interviews are often the source of company training. Trainers have mixed views on this. Some argue that it is an effective way of getting a summary of training needs to allow them to plan for the coming year. Others bemoan the fact that a shopping-list of training needs results from managers simply choosing from a list of available courses, as if course attendance is the only training solution available.

The best training is often on-job coaching by the manager. Other options include:

- Distance learning programmes (in-house, Open University programmes, etc)
- Short secondment to other departments
- Setting developmental projects overseen by the manager
- Shadowing a colleague or specialist manager
- Job-sharing.

Summary notes

Aim
The main aims of appraisal are to:

- Allow the subordinate to review their past year, and plan the next
- Provide honest praise and criticism where it is justified
- Help both manager and subordinate to improve their mutual support.

Planning
Plan your interview to meet your subordinate's wants and

needs as much as your own. If you are planning an appraisal in the near future:

- List the employee's wants and needs.
- List your wants and needs.
- List the 'behaviours' that will help the interview to meet both sets of needs.
- Review your subordinate's performance against last year's targets, getting opinions from other managers or supervisors if appropriate.
- Draft your objectives for their next year's work; ask yourself if you are satisfied with their performance this year or if they need to develop further.
- Do the objectives meet your interviewee's long-term needs, and those of the organisation?
- Review any training or development they may need to achieve the targets.

Preparation
- Give adequate notice to the interviewee.
- Invite them to prepare for the interview.
- Provide copies of any relevant forms.
- Choose a place where the interview will not be interrupted.
- Remind them of the interview a few days before it.

Structure
- Put your interviewee at ease.
- State the purpose of the interview.
- Give your overall impression of their work and progress.
- Explain the structure you will follow.
- Gain agreement to the purpose and structure.
- Ask for any comments but stick to your purpose; postpone discussion of short-term items.
- Discuss progress against last year's targets.
- Congratulate where appropriate; discuss weaknesses without embarrassment.
- Ask about any long-term ambitions and enthusiasms.
- Discuss and agree the assessment section of the appraisal

form; next year's targets; any training or development and
the objectives and training sections of the appraisal form.
- Sum up and agree the date of the next long-term appraisal.

Follow-up
- Arrange further interviews to discuss any short-term items
that arose.
- Ensure that training and development opportunities are
taken up.
- Check on general job performance.
- Watch for points of improvement and congratulate if
appropriate.
- Review your own performance and management style in
the light of any comments from appraisees (particularly if
several make similar comments).

CHAPTER 10
The Exit Interview

Making the most of 'goodbye'

Staff leaving an organisation are a valuable source of genuine feedback for any manager. Those who leave voluntarily have a chance to offer constructive and frank criticism that is not always possible for those continuing in employment.

Your organisation may have a 'leaver's form' or questionnaire for leavers, but the information gathered from these is often superficial and rarely proves useful. The best information for you as a manager are the home truths that may not be revealed in impersonal questionnaires. In fact, it will take a sensitive and mature approach to obtain them in a productive exit interview.

Even those who are, or appear to be, leaving for obvious reasons can provide useful information for you. The exit interview is best conducted in a relaxed manner, and adopting a near-counselling style. Gain the trust and then the genuine impressions of the leaver. If sensitively handled, exit interviews can be productive even in cases of redundancy. If you suspect there may be some bitterness in the air, you could ask a personnel officer or your manager to conduct the interview.

Aim
- To improve the selection process.

- To identify organisational problems.
- To reduce staff turnover.
- To dissuade the employee from leaving (if appropriate).
- To improve the image of the organisation in the mind of the leaver.

Planning

- Consider the individual leaver, and decide your aim for the interview (particularly if you wish to dissuade them from leaving).
- Remember that it is their views that matter at this stage, not yours.
- Be prepared to listen, and not react; the most useful criticism can be the hardest to swallow.
- Remember counter-criticism, or justification of past events, is of even less use here than in other interviews.

Preparation

- Research the leaver's work history.
- Examine the evidence for the expressed (or hidden) reason for resigning.
- Speak to the leaver's supervisor or other managers.
- Reflect on what you know of their personal background.

Structure

- Welcome the leaver and put them at ease.
- Express regret at their resignation.
- Explain your purpose for the interview.
- Ask 'open specific' questions about their reasons for leaving.
- Use probing questions to clarify detail, even if the facts are unwelcome.
- Avoid defending the organisation, but correct any errors of fact or policy.
- Make notes of any serious criticisms.
- Explain what you will do as a result.
- Offer thanks and good wishes.

Follow-up
- Revise the leaver's job description if required.
- Act on the notes you have made of any criticisms.
- Review the morale of those in similar positions.
- Report any serious matters to your manager.

Case study
Motivating professionals

Peter, the manager of a head office section of a large government department, appointed three new staff expressly to bring in some new ideas and a more professional approach to the work of the department. Three good candidates were found, but within nine months one of them, Brian, had resigned to go to a slightly less well paid job. The other two did not seem much better motivated but said little.

Peter interviewed Brian as soon as he gave his notice. Brian explained that far from welcoming fresh ideas, the section supervisor had constrained and frustrated the newcomers, allowed them little initiative in their work, and acted as though he felt threatened by them. Peter asked Brian to spend his last week writing a report on his impressions. Even allowing for Brian's personal bias, his report helped Peter to counsel the supervisor and review the selection process for a replacement. It also showed how easy it was for the supervisor to hide from Peter the daily realities in the section. Using the information he interviewed the other two new staff and was able to dissuade one who was thinking of leaving too.